Cicada Chimes

Helen Koukoutsis
Cicada Chimes

Acknowledgements

'Funeral' – *Nebu[lab]* (2010)
'Orthodox plot 223' – *A Little Poetry* (2013)
'Dad' – *fourW* twenty-seven (2016)
'Waiting for the 412' – Studio Showcase Prize; appeared in the Studio Showcase edition of *Studio: a journal of Christians' writing* (2014)
'Sophia' – *Communion* (2016)
'November twilight – 2009' – *Poetrix* (2011)
'At Serres train station' – *Marguerite Avenue* (2012)
'Paris – 2010' – *Marguerite Avenue* (2012)
'Easter poem' – *Studio: a journal of Christians' writing*
'3 a.m.' – *Buddhist Poetry Review* (2012)
'2007' – *Nebu[lab]* (2010)
'Sunday service at St Sophia's, Bourke Street Surry Hills' – *Poetry Quarterly* (2014)

The warmest thanks to Sarah and Jenny – friends, writers, colleagues – who read and commented on the manuscript many times, and to family, here and abroad, who read individual poems with keen interest. The biggest thanks to my husband Michael, whose love and encouragement were the driving force of this collection.

Cicada Chimes
ISBN 978 1 76041 403 0
Copyright © text Helen Koukoutsis 2017
Cover: Cicada © Steve Lovegrove

First published 2017 by
Ginninderra Press
PO Box 3461 Port Adelaide 5015 Australia
www.ginninderrapress.com.au

Contents

Funeral	7
Orthodox plot 223	9
Dad	14
Waiting for the 412	17
On the road to Rookwood	20
Impossible	23
Sophia	26
Hours	27
November twilight – 2009	29
Emily's loaded gun	32
At Serres train station	34
Through the lens	36
Paris – 2010	39
Easter poem	41
On vacation	44
3 a.m.	46
4 a.m.	49
Market day	54
2007	59
Sunday service	60
Forget I	64
The longest day	66

For my mother, and in loving memory of my late father

Funeral

They arrived
with a suitcase
3 cents
in their pockets
organically fed livers
and the hope of returning
home wealthy –
so their stories went
when I was growing up.

Twenty
thirty
forty years on
they surrender
their medically
prescribed bodies
to foreign soil. They
crave no more
for the old land
or the families
they left behind –
they wonder no more
when or how they'll die
or even if their pseudo-
Orthodoxy
will resurrect them.

Today
another's to be buried –
name carved into
priceless marble
not yet weathered
by a caustic sun –
he waits.

Just this once
I try to specialise
his absence
with an austere
performance
of the cross

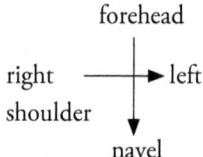

and just like
a compass
on the moon
my presence
among the
frankincense
and myrrh
seems pointless.

Orthodox plot 223

1

Memorial Avenue –
wasteland
of muted graves
PO box crematoriums

black
marble monuments
with inscriptions etched
in gold.

>   Crows caw
>   back and forth
>   from the tops
>   of ghost gums

2

I want to pull into the car park café
order cinnamon toast
spy on coffee drinkers.

I want to smile at the girl
in a blue dress and satin sash
trying to swallow whole
a muffin. But

aren't they ashamed
interrupts like gunfire
from the passenger seat.

She wants to say more
but she made the sign
of the cross
as we drove
through the gates.

Even the car radio
was hushed.

> A crow echoes
> mid-flight
> with short
> successive
> eh-awes.
> Whip-crack wings
> pull up and up

3

I wonder –
what about
the spinach pitas
the aniseed biscuits
olives, coffee
on doily napkins
at Dad's wake?

That's tradition
she'd say, and
why do you
always argue
with me?

>   The cacophony
>   swells –
>   noisy miners
>   cockatoos
>   magpies

The only
one still grieving
is Mum

and she's never
liked cafés
never sits in one
hates those who do –
and I don't always
argue with you.

4

Orthodox plots –
rusted bicycle
leans against
a row of conifers.

Dad
gets harder to find.

His headstone's
a granite ghost.
Black lithochrome
once exposed name
dates, an epitaph.

Only a tiny portrait
featuring his sideburns
resists the sun.

5

Mum pretends
to know the way
until she takes
a wrong turn.

Over here, Ma!

Her calico bag
is split
at the seam.

She likes it
that way.

In an instant –
out spills
oil, wick
frankincense.

>   Cicadas swell
>   like voices
>   in a choir

Dad

When the afternoon sun
settles on the mandarin tree
in Mum's backyard
I can see him standing
there by the open buds
posing for a snapshot
he'll never see. He's 50 –
wears a cable-knit jumper
brandless jeans.
On his temples –
the first signs of grey.
Slices of bread, kasseri
in one hand
salami in the other –
his hunger tamed
after a long day of mowing.

In the garden
he was Odysseus:
long-enduring
sharp
like the clippers he used
to trim grass edgings
or prune his fruit trees.
In public
he was Wile E. Coyote
chasing after the migrant dream:
job, house
education for his children.
His acme
was Wilhelm Reich's
Listen, Little Man –
his sole reading material
(except for the *Hellenic Herald*) –
the only book he read aloud
to his family as instruction.
He spoke little English
said *fuckteenia* a lot, *tsirkula ki*
for laughs (got many
from his friends
none from mine)
and smoked
Peter Stuyvesants
most of his life.

Twenty-five years on
I still see him
in hospital –
pensive
like a monk
on his daily fast –
and yet, the urgency
of his last kisses
on my trembling face –
Mum's steady hands

Waiting for the 412

I remember Mum's magnetic hands –
they'd coil tightly around the handle
of her vinyl trolley, mine
around grocery-filled plastic bags
that'd cut to the bone. I'd have been 17
maybe 18
standing at the bus stop
waiting for the 412 to arrive; but

I've also been 5 and at 5
we'd be at the Glomesh factory in Lewisham
picking up rolls of brilliant mesh
Mum was trusted to shape
into 100 handbags.

She had one week, one chore
one awl to slice mesh with.

On rainy days she'd take me to work –
lower me into the trolley. I'd crouch in darkness
like a Greek in a Trojan horse –
imagine the world outside
my enemy as she pulled me up stairs
and across train platforms. Her grasp –
like a cushion through the bumps
and depressions of asphalt.

At home
she'd work out of a 3 x 2 metre shed.
Fingers would curl tightly
around the awl as though around
an ink-black pen that told a story
(except, she never learned to read
or write, never learned to tell stories).
Before the first pierce
she'd perform her cross three times –
end briefly with palm on heart.

She'd live on Greek coffee, sleep 1 a.m.
earn 75 cents a bag – proud
she would gross more in a week
than her carpenter husband.

When he died, her hands were 53 –
juggling Endep and Stelazine
like a professional drug addict.
She'd manage the mortgage payments
balance the weekly budget with no math
and haul groceries with her trolley
for years
without him.

She was 56 the first time her hands
failed to hold her weight when she slipped
fell at the cemetery (we were arguing) –
      60 the first time
they trembled involuntarily
(*tardive dyskinesia*
her therapist would later say) –
      62 when they cramped up
kneading bread dough.

Now, at 76, old breakages haunt her
in the form of arthritis. Painkillers –
from time to time –
relieve.

I'm almost 40.

We never talk about those days
we waited for the 412 to steer us home
her vinyl trolley, the hundreds of handbags –
now vintage on eBay – she crafted
with an awl. We talk instead about my car
that always needs a clean
her colour-coded collection
of enviro bags, and forced retirement.

On the road to Rookwood

It's hard to believe
she's in the car with me.
She's so silent. Usually
she has a glory box
of random sentences
half-formed on her tongue
nothing special
mostly gripes about
>the past
>the old country
>the old ways
>her mother –

details reported
like the feature piece
on CNN or ERT news:
woke at dawn to milk cows
baked 15 breads for 8 siblings
bedridden mother, goat herder
father, displaced from village
to village like a refugee.

Today –
can't get used to her pulse
it drums prosaic alongside
honkers tailgaters drivers
who weave in and out of traffic.
Is it because we're on our way
to the cemetery? Is it because
I snapped at her earlier?
(Tired of hearing, *you're late*
just woke up?)

A BMW cuts me off
                            Meeeeep!
I give the driver the finger.
Not even the usual, tsk tsk tsk.
She's a Spartan severe a stoic martyr.
(After Arria stabbed herself
the words to her husband
relieved, *see, Paetus, it doesn't hurt…*
but it *must* hurt.)

Ahead –
man staggers
across intersection –
dodges cars and trucks
                            Toot toot toot tooooot!
makes it to the other side
only to collapse:
heart attack?
epilepsy?

Are you upset with me?
I get a half nod. Nestled
between her feet, basil
bunched together
with roses and dahlias.
They wait their usual arrangement
on Dad's grave.

Woman changes lanes –
no indicator –
just misses a chopper.
                            Honk honk!

Another rolls by
mobile in hand
texting –
husband?
babysitter?
lover?

                              Scrreeeech BANG!
Traffic stops. Exhaust
fills the air. In the distance
tires melt colloidal into concrete.
An accident.

The BMW that cut me off
has advanced two car spaces.
                              Beeeeeeeep!

She must know that I rely on her
to massage these klaxon moments
with perfect disparagement…

world's gone mad!

And there it is.

Impossible

Growing up
I was Anne of Green Gables –
all imagination

>sisters, instead of a brother
>who'd threaten me
>with tungsten darts

>fairies, instead of monsters
>who'd scurry like cockroaches
>when I'd switch on bedroom lights

>short, instead of long hair
>(Mum thought conditioners too pricy)
>red, like Anne's, instead of brown

>Jesus, instead of God –
>too impossible
>to pray to every night –
>I already had a Father.

Later
Emily Dickinson –
shut up in prose
writing a thesis

Dad gone –
God still too impossible.
Mum sang melancholy
Greek songs
by the laundry basin –
elbow high in suds. Afternoons –
she'd pluck her moustache
with old needle-nose pliers
Dad had used around the house –
she'd gaze into my hand-held Smurf mirror –
                sold to Dad for 250 drachma
                by a gypsy with Medusa hair.
                  (I was 11; Greece was home) –
count cat-like whiskers
glued to her reflection.

Now
Plath –
shut up in a gas stove
cooking three meals
a day
for a husband
not used to leftovers
and a daughter
who prefers
only toast.

Vefa's Kitchen
by the cooktop
Woolf on the nightstand – God
like a mark on the wall.

Sophia

Before martyrdom
you were Roman nobility – mother
of three daughters burnt, boiled
beheaded by Hadrian's underlings
in the name of the goddess – Artemis.

Before motherhood
you were a father's dowry – wife
in *stola* with wide-plaited hem
and gold embroidered sandals –
perpetually pregnant to a husband
three times your age
who died without an heir.

Before wifehood
you were betrothed – maiden
from the hills of Rome.
Your father's vineyard –
a playground –
the ooze and musket smell
of fallen grapes imprinted
deep in the frictions
on your fingers.

Before maidenhood – a girl
with curls – waist long –
educated by a devout mother.
Paul's virtues fixed like a bolt
on your third eye.
Never to be a citizen of this world.
Never to write your own laws.

Hours

Exit – hospital ward.
Bleach fumes follow her
into the elevator
down to the ground floor
out to the bus stop
into the bus –

> 40 minutes – alone
> on the back seat – baking in
> February heat through
> a dirty window – ant
> under a magnifying glass –
> in school uniform –
> waist-length braid –
> F – on this morning's maths test –
> crush on the school captain –
>
> *ding*!
>
> stand, ride
> the last 50 metres
> gripping onto a hot pole –

she steps
out onto the footpath
into the front garden
onto the veranda
past marigolds roses begonias
through the front door
into her mother's house
where saturation begins
bathrooms
bedrooms
kitchen
curtains
carpet
mind –
he's going to die –

November twilight – 2009

Cicada chimes
November twilight –
a hungry stillness
infuses the air
with perfumes
from summer's green-
house. Eucalyptus
and jasmine
like guitar string
serenade
nature's lovers.

>7.24 p.m.
>A quick glance at
>Google's thermometer –
>36°C, still. Dinner ended
>fifteen minutes ago. Got to get back
>to tap tap…taptaptaptap tap –
>trying to bring
>this poem home –

Birds emulate the nearby
suburban landscape –
clackety-clack trains
whooshing cars
on hot midnight asphalt.
Salted humidity wells up…
Salted humidity wells up…

> <u>7.33 p.m.</u>
> *Hun, what do you want me to do*
> *with the mayonnaise jar?*
>
> *Rinse it, for the recycle bin.*
>
> Will need to trek outside
> again. The tenth time today.
> He hasn't quite worked out
> what can and can't be recycled…
>
> in my mouth!

Salted humidity wells up
in my mouth. It's 36°C.
I am 36.
I am the Cooee bird that
cries out in the distance
at the violet sky, the sparrow
that falls from its nest
defeated…

> <u>7.45 p.m.</u>
> Can't write
> any more in this
> heat
>
> can't
> think.

In my left ear –
plates, pans, glassware
clink and rattle like chains around necks.
These are the last movements
in *Dar es Salaam*. He's
almost finished
with the dishes
and I am still
trying to
write

———

I open up a window.
The refrigerator motor
kicks into hum mode
the south wind bursts through.
There will always be dishes to clean
and waste to recycle, but this poem,
tonight, must live forever unfinished

Emily's loaded gun

Quick!
Toss me Emily's
loaded gun. I have
a migraine and the boy
on his chainsaw chariot,
who rides the neighbourhood
asphalt, ignites in me
Vesuvius.

When he isn't
circling the block
he's outside my door
smoking bongs in a car
with four other teenagers.
The next morning –
condoms, chocolate wrappers
in the gutter.

Some days he waits
for a gold Mercedes.
Some days it comes
jet-ski in tow; tinted windows
reflect a suburban landscape.
Last night, he lodged
a porn video
in my mail box…

the gun, please. I need
to swallow whole
thick phlegm – hot
in the back of my throat –
which oozes yellow
drip
drip

calls itself the flu,
carpets the mouth red
with ulcers. A single shot
to mangle nerves
10 hours silence
sleep –
the gun. Or,

let his dealer
raze his body
to the sound
of lawnmowers
hammers, drills,
for only his dealer
has the power to kill
without the power to die.

At Serres train station

We sit at a lamplit tavern
on the edge of Serres –
famous for its soccer team
Tuesday morning markets
custard-filled pastries sprinkled
with cinnamon and icing sugar –
made by lemon-breasted women
in headscarves who master
the basics of rolling dough at ten.

An empty bottle of *Tsiporo*
and half-eaten *mezzes* amplify
my impending departure. An order
of coffee, on its way. In a few days
I'll be back in Sydney –
another parting to write about.

I used to wear your hand-me-downs
and listen to your Led Zeppelin cassettes
like I was learning a foreign language.
Now you're a grandmother. At 37
I'm yet to be a mother.

Even the coffee's *kaimaki* (froth)
opens into a black hole.

Coffee is meditation here, the soul
it cannot be drunk in a hurry. So
we drink, slowly, to health –
mosquitoes feast on our blood.
It's 9.30 p.m. The last train from Thessalonica
whistles into the station
bringing travellers home.

Through the lens

1

Old country, old ways –
lives still depend on
yiayia's red wheelbarrow.

Two 60-year-old sisters
study doily patterns –
compare cross stitches.

First in season –
green grapes hang
outside my uncle's shed.

Black and white pictures of Dad
in his army suit –
no visible wrinkle.

Aunts demand *eat, eat* –
just as bossy
as when I was eleven.

Pelicans
face the sunset –
nests atop telegraph poles.

Another night
another bed –
same mosquitoes.

2

Russo-Pontian apartments
by a motorway –
mansion ghettos.

Albanian boys
zigzag through tavern tables –
food money coupons.

Outside
a Thessalonican bakery –
gypsy woman breastfeeds.

Asian dress shop
in Serres –
empty of customers.

My 9-year-old niece
holds me back –
we don't go in there; we only buy Greek.

Bulgarians 'trespass'
on the back of rusty utes –
will work for 5 euro.

Cousins uncles aunts
ride the bus to Sofia –
cheap nuts dates feta.

3

Roupel –
Mum's birth village –
only Agios Demetrious still stands.

Paris – 2010

On the river Seine
a calm liquid breeze
sweeps the peaks of the old cathedral.
It's the last day of June. Girls
in three-quarter jeans
hang out with boys
by the banks of the river.
They wait for the night to begin –
cheer, blow kisses at us as though we're kin.
They do it to please us –
'cause we're tourists
and crave entry into their world.

Amidst the cheers, *vive la France*!
can be heard: a young boy
or girl, perhaps.

I think of the countless tolls
we paid to get here; the gypsies
we ignored at the base of the Eiffel
with their luring letters from home.
I think of the graffiti we saw
on the walls of unkempt buildings – illegible
except for the occasional *fuck*. I wonder
how they can climb so high, why they bother.
I remember today's headlines
on some Parisian newspaper:
Sarkozy supports burqa ban.

I snap a long shot of their faces.
He snaps a silhouette
of the old cathedral
through the reflection
of the cruise boat window –
the rays of the orange sunset
slice through its peaks.
It's a city of 160 Catholic churches.
The announcement comes
through the microphone.
He snaps –
he snaps again.
Just-married is graffitied on his face
on every digitised image of my face.

Easter poem

Another Resurrection on the street
listening to the congregation snort
at ushers, queue jumpers, teenagers
with iPhones, rising candle prices
coin-collectors who count clinks
with suspicious eyes. It's 11.40 p.m. –
too late to secure a seat inside
too cloudy to enjoy the moon, the stars.

This year, girls in black dresses
and high heels wear make-up –
boys in suit jackets, as young as 5
wear hair gel. The only party they'll attend,
following tonight's service, will include
a bowl of lemony-green soup made from
lamb's guts and liver, red-dyed eggs –
hardboiled – and *yiayia*'s whiskery kisses.
She'll stay up late and tell stories
about the old country, to rolling eyes.

In the thickening crowd, a little girl
appears agitated – dimpled fingers
crank round the ribbon on her candle.
She's been waiting for the priest
to emerge from his cave of shadows
but like the others, who arrive late
and stand outside, the wait
takes place in something
resembling Dante's vestibule. Limbs
fall prey to stings and bites –
Mummy, my legs hurt.
Not much longer to go, sweetie.
Mother's voice is tender, persuasive.
Inside
the priest signs 'God is love'
on the minds of every sinner
with faded ink and incense.
His voice trembles through
the loudspeaker. The Paschal Vigil
culminates in a brief litany
before surrounding lights are extinguished.

I come for the ritual –
we all do:
the sight of the holy flame
as it multiplies to hundreds thousands millions
the resounding bell at midnight
the song, *Christ is risen from the dead*, chanted 12 times.
Fireworks graffiti the night sky. You'd think it's New Year's.
Candles glow resplendent under milky street lights –
they motion through darkness like electric ghosts.

It's needed, this ritual –
we cannot get into our cars and drive home
we cannot burn the cross above our doorways
we cannot eat our lamb's guts and liver soup
without the belief that God watches our every move.

On vacation

It's 2 a.m. on the shores of Chalkidiki.*
We're wide awake, my cousin and I
insomniacs stranded beneath a diamond sky.

Siren waves roll in from the Aegean.
Like a snow cornice on the crest of a mountain
they break. Our voices break with them.

This is Macedonia: marbled, Olympian.
Mount Athos to the left where no woman
may enter. The Meteora to the right suspended

like gods. To the north of where we sit
a small mosquito-infested village crammed
with cornfields cousins uncles aunts.

In a week's time we'll be north sampling
siestas on my *yiayia*'s divan; lentil soup
in the mornings, watermelon and feta in the evenings.

No wrinkles on our faces, none on our hands
no children, no husbands to contest our philosophies –
my first solo odyssey away from home.

Except, I am a tourist discovering a people
whose idle ways have been shaped by centuries
of occupation – someone who likes to read

Homer for leisure and study the language
long after the imposition of Greek school
for the sake of parents who never learned

to speak English well. Their voices migrated
thousands of miles away where no gods
no cliff-faced monasteries, no family existed.

They made friends with fellow compatriots
worked in glass and nappy factories, earned 15c an hour.
Half their weekly wages supported parents back home.

With one eye fixed on a better life, the other
on their roots, it would take them decades
to realise that home is just geography.

My cousin says *the anchor releases only in wisdom*.
She's been reciting Cavafy all night, but
I'm on vacation and home is a million miles away.

* pronounced phonetically: 'hul-ki-thi-ki' – the 'c' is silent.

3 a.m.

Hot, angry clots
charge through
crimson loins –
you've just expelled
a lentil. Contractions
suggest otherwise.
Blood and lining
anchor on
to the early hours
of the morning –
life
death
84 heartbeats –
the outcome
was settled before
conception. There's
nothing you can do
crumpled over
a bloated belly –
ass suspended
like a drawbridge.

You plan
to do it right
next time –
eat right
sleep right
walk right
like the Buddha.

You promise to guard
your mind against
negative thoughts –
37-year-old uterus
(cysts, polyps
endometriosis)
food intolerances
that never existed
as a kid. You
vow to avoid
the internet
random superstitions
and social beliefs
of the kind that assume
all women dive
naturally
into motherhood.
Most of all
you promise
never to write
about this
because inside
the bowl of waste
and water
an embryo has fallen
like a sparrow
from its nest –

it will never
know sound
sight
taste
its own bitter
demise –
it will never know
how to spell
this moment
or offer
a comforting voice
when you look back
and see this –
another loss.

4 a.m.

It's become a habit
to reach for kettle
and chamomile at 4 a.m. –
sugar pill
for carpal tunnel
and burning rash
on swollen belly.
Can't get any bigger, she thinks,
dropping two tea bags
into a Country Road mug
like the ones her mum would buy
at Brennan's department store
when she was 9.
They weathered
the move back to Greece
without fracture.

In Greece
blood turned to wine
school was 9 months a year –
summer: countryside and cousins
visiting relics of saints in churches
and wax effigies of sinners
in Vrellis' museum.
Greece was meant to be forever.
Forever lasted a year;
it was broken Brennan's mugs
borrowed money, Italian
velvet sofas preserved in plastic
shipped to Port Botany
for collection on return;
it was her father's tears
as he parted again
from his old man:
Greek Civil War survivor
who once used his walking stick
to beat his wife and children.

                                    Her father –

                                    never afraid
                                    of anything
                                    except cancer
                                    and freeway driving

                                    never to be a grandfather.

At the dining table
in her husband's house
she thinks about her mother –
suburbs away, alone on her divan
reading her history book of regrets –
waiting for her first grandchild.

And she thinks about the garden:
weeds bloom, snails feast on dahlias.
She hasn't used *Blitzem*
in two years. Not
since her mother-in-law
said she should – said, too,
in the same breath
across the same table
in the same house
I hate Jews. No reason.
just do.

At another table
in another house
middle-aged uncles
at family gatherings
smoked Marlboros
and drank whiskey till 1 a.m.
21 in the lounge
with corduroy couch covers
Mikis Theodorakis
on the record player –
they would talk about going home
to be with the Greeks, and yet
their only friends here
spoke Greek
thought in Greek
were born
and certified Orthodox Greek.
Most dead, now. Her father –
the first to go.
And with him, too,
family gatherings.

In the distance
the motorway hums, a train
passes: factory workers –
plastics rubber glass.
48 hours from now
she'll be on that motorway
on her way to hospital –
some other woman
pregnant at 4 a.m.
will sip chamomile
and contemplate the family
her daughter will be born into.

Market day

5 a.m.
tents are set.
7 a.m. the cries begin –
Three Euro! With three Euro
Italy has come to Greece, girls.
Nothing Chinese!
Nothing Greek either.

Marketers yell for hours.
Women, children
sleep in nearby apartments –
husbands, fathers
labour in fields till sundown
between long siestas.

Behind the food stall
a family of crows squawk –
too early for leftovers.

Three Euro won't buy the buckle
of an Italian calfskin leather bag;
at Serres markets
it buys buckle bag shoes. No one
takes note of 'Genuine Lather' tags
except Litsa. She teaches English
at the local *Frontistirio*
like most Greek-Brits
who come for the summer
and never leave.

Low-rise jeans, singlet top
the whale tail of her G-string sways
like a dinghy in the ocean
as she saunters from stall to stall –
flip flops clap clap calloused soles.
In Serres, she acts herself.
She can be on her fourth coffee
her one millionth cigarette
without the threat of some packet-advert
telling her she'll die from the addiction
and orphan her daughter.

At Mario's stall
she picks at bags and purses
strewn on a makeshift table.
She's not alone.
Ten other women grope around
for the perfect-life-as-a-bag –
dream of groping Mario's Herculean body.
His rust-dyed beard
hangs loose to his chest;
his head, newly shorn –
not because it's summer
but because he's balding –
bears the heat like an icy pole.
He'd rather be on a beach in Thasos
with his girlfriend, or on his chopper
riding through Corfu's cobbled streets –
he'd rather be a waiter, shelf filler, drug dealer, anything
than listen to one more haggler –

usually male shopping cheap
for his mistress or wife –
drive his prices down.
Come on, Mario!
I'm giving you 2 Euro
don't ask for extra.
For six years
he's been selling women's bags
to make ends meet. He's heard it all
except *Italika dermatina? Sovara?*
Litsa's accent is broken.
She dangles a bag.
'Genuine Lather' tags
exposed like sly
slip of the tongue politicians.

He finds her suspicion amusing
her ass rhythmic like a metronome.

He's seen her around town –
cotton-blonde hair, legs that tower to heaven.
He remembers Independence Day
by the statue of Emmanuel Pappas –
his wink at her, which she ignored.

SO-VA-RA! He mocks her accent.
The women burst into loud guffaws –
no time for apologies.
Litsa throws the bag onto the pile
walks off, mutters
the same slang term
she once heard cockneys use
at the College pub back home,
fuckin' squeaks.
They stare at her as she disappears
around the corner –

Platia Eleftherias – ahead –
her teenage daughter
in their one-bedroom apartment
above the markets –
asleep.

She walks.

Gia sou, Litsa!
A wave and wink
for the three old men
who take all day
to drink a cup of coffee
at the local Kafenio.

They wait for her
salivate over her
follow her
with watery red-rimmed eyes.
She doesn't mind –
prefers men wrinkled
and smelling of rolled-up cigarettes
than Aramis or Hugo Boss.

On Leof. Merarchias
two shopfronts covered
in thick red print: *closing down sale, all half price*.
A woman begs for change
outside the Millennium bank –
just lost her home. Litsa ignores her.
The corner kiosk displays
the front page of *Nea Epochi*:
Suicide Crisis in Serres.
Crisis, what crisis? Litsa parrots the locals.
To lie to mock to steal –
the way of life here
even in a small town like Serres that sleeps
through heat and market criers.

She walks.

The whale tail of her G-string sways
like a dinghy in the ocean. She walks.

Her ass rhythmic
like a metronome.

2007

This country
they call
Greece
these people –

>their philosophy –
>the angry expression
>on civil servants
>who ignore you
>on approach –
>the hubris
>of crop farmers –
>the arrogant young –

the smell of Camel cigarettes
in airports, banks, and cafeterias –
of burning Peloponnesian forests –

I could (not) have lived
without seeing them all
this summer

Sunday service

Leather-skinned men
in grey suits count donations
behind a door – ajar –
St Sophia's darkest corner
where we huddle
to lull our baby's screams –
close to the clinks
of the collection box –
the furthest point
from the altar.

My husband calls
the leather-skinned men
accountants. He should know
he's one himself. We watch them
through the crack in the door:
four, five around a table
count
mutter
confer borrowed gifts.

A dwarfish man – fat –
squeezes past.
Our baby erupts in tears.
He excuses himself, fondles
the brass door knob
adjusts his balls
enters the room.
He shuts the door.
On his left pinkie
a ring – gold –
the kind my dad wore:
embossed Acropolis
with a teeny ruby for a sun.
He aspired to become a cantor – Dad did
not the dwarf I've never met
who's *a benefactor*
my husband whispers in my ear.

Of what? I whisper back.
Of St Sophia's – the Church
not the martyr; *he raises
revenue through charities.*
How does my husband know so much?

Men, more men enter
through the door
clones of the first:
short, stocky, in grey.
One returns with a candle
lights it, performs his cross
kisses several icons.
Barrel-belly concealed
behind a black pinstriped suit.

An usher approaches him
mumbles something –
they smile. Then us.
Cheshire cat eyes
spy our daughter:
here for communion?
No I whisper
she's unbaptised.
The usher's eyelids droop
Garfield-like.
His lanky march
steers him to the door.
Hand jiggles the knob –
foreplay. He enters.
Inside: will he tell?
We three stand
at the narthex
of St Sophia's.

Jesus gazes
from his sanctuary.
Gold gilded halo.
He's a long way
from Jerusalem –
a long way from Temple
Passover, money changers –
and yet
and yet –

Auxiliary women –
pear-shaped in pencil skirts
nylon calves and beehives –
carry cheques with a smile
through the door.
I glance at my husband –
our daughter asleep in his arms.
Bake offs, tea parties he whispers
*they raise money for the Church
and the poor*. What he doesn't know
is that they'll never be
one of the men (entering
exiting through that door
like they own the space).
No mother
daughter
sister
will ever be in St Sophia's –

not even Sophia?

Forget I

1

A solitary dragonfly peek-a-boos me
from behind rusted rail lines.

No squeal or clackety-clack
of steel-impending-wheels threaten its dance.

After all, what does it know about trains
and schedules that keep little rhythm?

Consider its mosaic wings: tiny tornado swirls
graffiti the morning light in fast forward.

2

I follow the dance
for one split second
I forget

he's dead.

I forget
my panic –

the impulse
to cry.

I forget the 6 a.m. buzzer –
the eight minute sprint to the station
the hour-long journey to work –

my lunch
on the kitchen table –

half-empty classroom –

teaching *Hamlet* for the 100th time
on chocolate energy.

I forget the train arriving
forget embarking
forget I
forget, too, the dragonfly.

The longest day

1. In the beginning you created
the heaven and the earth.
2. And your face brooded
over the waters of the deep.
3. And you summoned the light,
the fowls, all creeping things, and me.
4. And we came. We tunnelled
through the molten darkness –
newborns fenced with bones, cartilage,
fashioned with flesh.
5. And we waited.
6. I waited the l o n g e s t.
7. I let you stare into my nakedness
with the conviction of a self-possessed lover
that feeds among the lilies.
8. And you stared –
your left hand on my breast
your right on lips.
9. O 'thy love *was* better than wine'
and wilder than the spices in your garden.

2. The last time you smiled at me
with those sweet-smelling lips of myrrh
an embryonic heart died in your likeness.
2. My vineyard ceased its crops.
3. You wondered from prophet to prophet
spreading plagues, the Law, and leprosy.
4. You tested Job on his devotion,
Elijah on his convictions, and twice
protected Hagar from Sarah's jealousy.
5. Women suffered barrenness
for years before you submitted
with compassion. Only one woman –
6. Proved favourable. They say
she bore you a son who could cure
the lame, the blind, the mute, the bleeding.
7. And a bleeding woman thought
'if I may but touch his garment,
I shall be whole.'
8. And she was whole.
9. And she was clean.

3. What garment was there for me to touch?
2. What gall, for me to swallow?
3. Physicians, today, remove
disease for a small fee, but
the disease you left me with
no physician can incise and cure.
4. Month after month it's there
chewing on womb, like termite on tree.
5. I let you know this. You only say
Good wombs make good babies.
6. Except good babies may not
make good adults.
7. Oh, why was I not granted
Rebekah's assurance
though two nations split in her womb?
8. Or Ruth's craft at persuading her kinsman
to lie with her unwed?
9. Even Elisabeth, in her old age
received the Holy Ghost.

4. I tried so hard
to conceive without you –
appealed to Saint Sophia
and her daughters
for a child of my own.
2. They gave me a daughter
who can never be a saviour.
3. She can never be God.
4. My other lover recently
confessed, *I don't believe*
Jesus was God, either.
5. Or that he boasted
'I am the way, the truth, the life'
6. *And I don't believe*, he said,
that our unborn child
will be punished just because
I ironed on a holy day.
7. But he has not seen your wrath
your jealousy, the millions killed
in the Great Flood.
8. He does not know why
you give a loaf to every bird
but just a crumb to me.
9. Why, I tell myself,
this daughter I carry
may never restore me
from the embarrassment
of your unrequited love.

5. Is it you who disapproves
of me washing laundry on Fridays?
2. Or is it the old wife
whose prattling whiskers
rise and fall with every falsehood told?
3. Or the mother you gave me –
the mother who gave her to the world?
4. She insisted that your son
was crucified every Friday, so,
no sock, underwear, bra,
and trouser could be washed.
5. I can't imagine either one
of these women as embryos.
6. They live
while I die watching you
renovate the world
like an old-fashioned school ma'am.
7. And this daughter I carry
this lover I've married
will die, too,
someday
just like my father.
8. Is it you who implanted
this destiny in us?
9. Will you die with us, too,
you who echo 'I am that I am'?

10. And who is that exactly
if not your true beloved
who bows to your absence
like a thirsting dianthus
who prays to keep alive
her lover and child
longer than herself?

www.ingramcontent.com/pod-product-compliance
Lightning Source LLC
Chambersburg PA
CBHW062154100526
44589CB00014B/1834